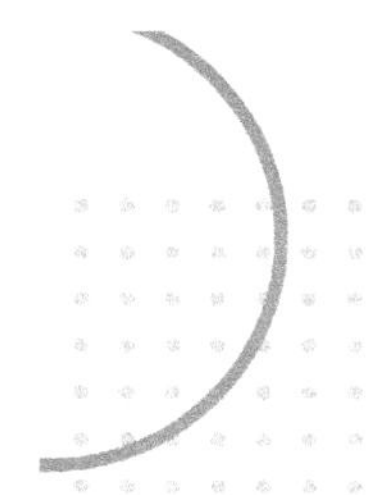

Table Of Contents

Contents

Baked Beans With Frankfurters

Ingredients

- 4 slices bacon cut in 1/2 -inch pieces
- 1/3 cup onions minced
- 1/3 cup celery minced
- 1 (21-ounce) can pork and beans in tomato sauce
- 1/3 cup ketchup
- 1 1/2 tablespoons molasses
- 3 tablespoons brown sugar
- Hot pepper sauce to taste
- Salt to taste
- 8 hot dogs all-meat sliced in half lengthwise, then crosswise

Procedure

Sauté bacon within a skillet. Add onion and celery make, stirring, until limp. Mix in coffee beans, ketchup, molasses, brown sugars, very hot pepper sauce, and salt to flavor. Simmer for five minutes. Include frankfurters and simmer, protected, for ten minutes, stirring occasionally.

Baked Beans With Ham Hock

Ingredients

- 4 cups navy beans cooked
- Meat from 1 ham hock, cubed
- 1 cup bean stock
- 1/2 cup onions minced
- 1/3 cup brown sugar firmly packed or to taste
- 1/4 cup ketchup
- 1 teaspoon dry mustard
- Salt to taste
- 2 tablespoons vegetable oil or fat from bean stock
- 1 teaspoon instant coffee
- 2 slices bacon cut into 1/2 -inch pieces and browned (optional)

Procedure

(For beans, ham hock, and bean stock components, please notice cooking food guidelines for Navy blue Coffee beans with the formula for Minestrone Soups Preheat stove to 325° Farrenheit. In a big saucepan, provide to boil coffee beans, cubed pig, share, onion, brownish sugars, ketchup, mustard, sodium, essential oil or excess fat, and quick espresso. Pour into a lightly greased 2-quart casserole and bake for 1 hr, mixing sometimes. Include even more water if required. Function capped with optionally available bacon items.

Baked Whiting With Shrimp Sauce

Ingredients

- 1 pound whiting sole, or turbot fillets
- 1 (10 1/2-ounce) can cream of shrimp soup
- 1 1/2 cups round buttery crackers crushed
- 1/4 cup margarine melted
- 1 tablespoon onions grated
- 1/2 teaspoon Worcestershire sauce
- 1/2 teaspoon hot pepper sauce
- 1 tablespoon lemon juice fresh

Procedure

Heat oven to 375° F. Location fillets in a greased shallow baking dish. Pass on soup over the best sprinkle with crushed crackers. Mix collectively margarine, onion, Worcestershire sauce, warm pepper sauce, and lemon fruit juice pour over crackers. Bake for 20 to 25 minutes, or until sizzling and bubbly and seafood flakes easily.

Note: Add 1/2 cup small shrimp to the sauce for a supplementary touch.

Beef And Vegetable Pie

Ingredients

- Meat tenderizer
- 1 pound beef round steaks cut in 1-inch cubes
- 3 tablespoons flour
- 1 1/2 tablespoons vegetable oil
- 1/2 cup onions sliced
- 1 teaspoon salt
- Freshly ground pepper to taste
- 1/2 teaspoon Worcestershire sauce
- 1 cup water
- 1 (8-ounce) can tomatoes whole
- 3 carrots small, cut in 2-inch julienne strips
- 2 potatoes medium pared and cut in 1-inch cubes
- Pastry for unbaked pie crust

Procedure

Sprinkle meat tenderizer more than beef cubes in accordance with guidelines. Roll cubes in 2 tablespoons flour. Heat essential oil in a heavy saucepan brown meat gradually. Add onion and cook until soft. Stir in staying 1 tablespoon flour, salt, pepper, and Worcestershire sauce. Mix in water makes, stirring, until thickened. Protect and simmer 30 minutes. Include tomatoes, carrots, and potatoes. Cover cook thirty minutes longer until meats and veggies are tender. Stir sometimes adds a little bit of drinking water if required. Pour right into a 10-in. Pie plate. Roll pastry to match the top of the pie plate. Help to make crosswise slits in middle and fold corners back again. Place over the best of the pie plate and flute edges. Bake in a preheated 425° F oven, 20 to 25 moments or until crust will be browned.

Broiled Tuna Burgers

Ingredients

- 1 (6 1/2-ounce) can tuna drained and flaked
- 2 tablespoons onions chopped
- 1/4 cup celery chopped
- 2 tablespoons sweet pickle relish
- 3 tablespoons mayonnaise real
- 3 hamburger buns split and toasted
- 3 to 4 tablespoons margarine
- 6 slices American cheese sharp

Procedure

Mix tuna, onion, celery, relish, and mayonnaise. Pass on hamburger buns with margarine best with tuna mixture. Best, each with a slice of cheese. Preheat stove broiler. Broil five ins from heat for four moments or until cheese melts.

Campers' Summer Sausage

Ingredients

- 5 pounds ground beef regular
- 3 1/2 teaspoons black pepper freshly ground
- 5 teaspoons salt quick-cure white
- 1 teaspoon garlic salt
- 1 teaspoon hickory smoke-flavored salt
- 2 tablespoons mustard seeds
- 1 tablespoon salt table

Procedure

Mix all ingredients properly in a big bowl and cover-up. Refrigerate every day and night. Mix well and refrigerate for yet another 48 hrs. Divide into 4 components shape into rolls for cookie rolls. Pour 1/2 cups water into the bottom part of broiler pan and location rolls of sausage on a rack over drinking water. Bake in a preheated 350° F stove for one hour. Cool store in the fridge or freeze.

Note: Floor beef with a lot of fat maintains this sausage moist. Good offered very hotly with new potatoes.

Charlie's Beef Stew

Ingredients

- 1 boneless beef chuck 1 1/2 - to 2-pound cubed and trimmed of all fat
- 1/4 cup vegetable oil
- 1 (10 1/2-ounce) can onion soup
- 1 (10 1/2-ounce) can cream of mushroom soup
- 1/4 cup burgundy wine

Procedure

Heat oven to 250° F. Brown types of meat in essential oil in a Dutch cooker or heavy oven pot. Mix collectively, the soups and wines pour over meat. Protect and bake for 5 hours, sometimes stirring—function over noodles or rice.

Note: Could be baked in 350° F for 3 hours or even until tender.

Cheese-Rice Soufflé

Ingredients

- 3 eggs separated
- 1 cup white rice cold cooked
- 1/2 cup milk
- 2 tablespoons margarine
- 4 ounces sharp cheddar cheese shredded
- dash salt

Procedure

Heat oven to 250° F. Brown types of meat in essential oil in a Dutch cooker or heavy oven pot. Mix collectively, the soups and wines pour over meat. Protect and bake for 5 hours, sometimes stirring—function over noodles or rice.

Note: Could be baked at 350° F for 3 hours or even until tender.

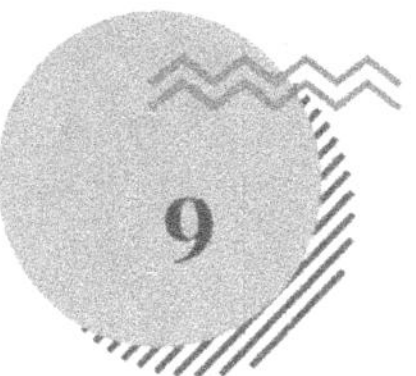

Cheese-Stuffed Manicotti With Meat Sauce

Ingredients

- 1 pound ground beef
- 1 tablespoon vegetable oil
- 1 tablespoon olive oil
- 1/2 cup onions chopped
- 1 garlic large, minced
- 2 (6-ounce) cans tomato paste
- 2 cups water
- 1 3/4 teaspoons salt
- Freshly ground pepper to taste
- 4 tablespoons parsley chopped fresh
- 4 teaspoons basil dried, crushed
- 3/4 pound ricotta cheese
- 1/3 cup Parmesan cheese grated
- 1 egg beaten
- 8 ounces manicotti shells
- parmesan cheese grated

Procedure

Brown beef in veggie and olive oils. Include onion, garlic, tomato paste, water, 1/2 teaspoons salt, pepper to taste, 2 tablespoons parsley, and basil. Simmer for 45 minutes, uncovered, stirring sometimes. In a bowl mix ricotta cheese, 1/3 mug Parmesan cheese, and egg include remaining 2 tablespoons parsley, 1/4 teaspoon salt, and pepper to flavor. Make manicotti in boiling salted drinking water until tender, drain wash in cold water. Utilizing a pastry bag, fill manicotti with cheese combination or slice lengthwise with scissors, open up, fill up, and reform. Pour one-half the tomato-meats sauce right into a 7 x 11-in . baking dish. Arrange stuffed manicotti in a coating, overlapping slightly. Best with staying sauce. Sprinkle with Parmesan cheese. Bake in a preheated 350° F oven for 25 to thirty minutes, basting occasionally.

Cheesy Chili Strata

Ingredients

- 5 to 6 slices bread (crusts removed), buttered and cut into cubes
- 3/4 pound longhorn cheese grated
- 1/2 pound pork sausages bulk pork sausage
- 4 eggs beaten
- 2 cups milk
- 1/2 teaspoon salt
- 1/2 teaspoon dry mustard
- 2 to 4 green chilies or to taste

Procedure

In a greased 8-inch sq . baking dish, location layers of a loaf of bread, cheese, sausage, and bread, respectively. Include eggs to milk, salt, and mustard blend nicely. Pour over bread best with green chilies. Protect and refrigerate overnight. Bake for 60 mins in a preheated 325° F oven cover up the last five minutes. Serve immediately.

Note: This recipe is most effective with day-old bread.

Chicken And Corn

Ingredients

- 6 eggs beaten
- 2 (10 1/2-ounce) packages frozen corn cooked and drained
- 8 ounces Muenster cheese finely diced
- 3 cups chicken cooked, cut in bite-size pieces
- 1 cup carrots sliced, cooked and drained
- 1 (10 1/2-ounce) package frozen green beans cooked and drained
- 1 (10 1/2-ounce) package peas frozen, cooked and drained
- 1 teaspoon salt
- Freshly ground pepper to taste
- 1/2 cup green olives pitted, sliced
- 2/3 cup chicken broth
- 1/4 cup golden raisins (optional)
- 2 tablespoons margarine
- 1 green bell pepper seeded and cut in strips
- 1 red bell pepper seeded and cut in strips, or 1 4-ounce jar whole pimiento, cut in strips

Procedure

Mix eggs, corn, and cheese inside a moderate bowl. In another dish, mix poultry, carrots, beans, peas, salt, pepper, olives, chicken stock, and optionally available raisins. Oil a shallow 3-quart baking meal place a layer of egg-corn mix in the bottom part. Add a coating of poultry mixture carries on alternating levels closing with a coating of egg-corn combination. Dot best with margarine garnish with switching pieces of green and red pepper or pimiento in a flowerlike style. Bake for 40 to 50 mins in a preheated 350° Farrenheit oven. Let are a symbol of ten minutes before helping.

Note: One 3 1/2 -lb chicken produces around 3 mugs meats. Veggies could be prepared in poultry broth for additional taste.

12

Chicken Crepes

Ingredients

- 1 broiler-fryer chicken double breasted cut up
- 1 carrot medium, sliced
- 1 onion medium, studded with 2 whole cloves
- 2 ribs celery sliced
- Few sprigs of fresh parsley
- 1 teaspoon salt
- 3 peppercorns whole
- 1/2 cup margarine
- 1/2 cup flour
- 4 1/2 cups chicken broth
- dash nutmeg of ground or to taste
- Salt and freshly ground pepper to taste
- 1 (5-ounce) can water chestnuts sliced, drained
- 16 to 20 crepes
- Paprika

Procedure

In a big kettle location, chicken, carrot, onion, celery, parsley, salt, and peppercorns. Add water to bring to boil. Reduce warmth, cover, and simmer softly for one hour or until poultry is tender. Remove poultry strain and measure share. There should be around 4 1/2 cups (boil down or add water to take it to that quantity if necessary). When the chicken has cooled, skin, bone, and slice into bite-size items. In a saucepan, melt margarine includes flour and cook, stirring, for three minutes. Add chicken stock slowly, stirring constantly make for ten minutes or until easy and thickened. Include nutmeg, salt, and pepper to flavor. Stir in drinking water chestnuts and poultry. Spoon three to four 4 tablespoons sauce onto the center of every crepe and roll-up. Arrange packed crepes in one layer in 2 9 x 13-in . baking dishes. Spoon staying sauce over crepes. Sprinkle with a dusting of paprika. Invest a preheated 325° F oven for 15 to 20 mins or until heated through.

Chicken Soufflé

Ingredients

- 1/4 cup margarine
- 1/4 cup flour
- 1 cup milk
- 1 teaspoon salt
- Freshly ground pepper to taste
- 1 cup chicken or 1 chicken breast, cooked and finely ground
- 6 eggs separated
- * Part two.
- 1 (10 1/2-ounce) can cream of mushroom soup
- 1/2 cup sour cream
- 2 to 3 tablespoons pimiento chopped

Procedure

Heat oven to 375° F. Melt margarine to mix in flour and prepare three minutes. Add milk progressively cook, stirring continuously, until sauce bubbles and thickens. Remove from warmth, add salt, pepper, floor chicken, and gently beaten egg yolks. Reserve. Defeat egg whites until stiff, however, not dried out. Fold into the chicken combination and spoon into an 8-in . square baking dish. Bake 35 moments or until the top is really a golden puff. Function at once with the next sauce.

Sauce:
*Heat soup in the saucepan. Mix in sour lotion and pimiento. Function with Chicken Soufflé.

Chicken Strata Divan

Ingredients

- 6 slices bread crusts removed
- 2 (10 1/2-ounce) packages frozen broccoli spears cooked and well-drained
- 3/4 pound sharp cheddar cheese grated or longhorn cheese
- 3 cups chicken cubed cooked or ham, or mixture of both
- 1 cup evaporated milk
- 2 1/2 cups chicken broth
- 6 eggs beaten
- 1/2 teaspoon salt
- 1 teaspoon dry mustard
- 2 tablespoons onions minced
- 12 slices bread cut into rounds
- Parmesan cheese Grated

Procedure

Place 6 whole bread slices in underneath of a greased 9 x 13-in . baking dish. with the broccoli layer with one-fifty percent of the cheese. Add meats and remainder of cheese. Combine milk, chicken stock, eggs, salt, mustard, and onion. Pour gently over layers. Top with bread rounds. Cover and invest refrigerator overnight. Bring to room temperature before baking in a preheated 325° F oven for 55 mins or until arranged. Sprinkle Parmesan cheese along with bread rounds carefully brown under broiler. Let set ten minutes before serving.

Chili

Ingredients

- 3 pounds ground beef
- 2 onions medium, chopped
- 2 cloves garlic minced
- 2 1/2 cups tomato juice
- 1 (16-ounce) can tomatoes whole, cut up and liquid reserved
- 2 (8-ounce) cans tomato sauce
- 1/4 cup chili powder
- 2 teaspoons salt
- 2 teaspoons oregano dried leaves
- 1 1/2 teaspoons cumin ground
- 2 (15-ounce) cans chili beans chili beans in gravy
-

Procedure

Set in a big skillet or Dutch oven over medium-high heat, cook and stir beef, onions, and garlic until meats are brown and onions are tender pipe off fat.

Stir in tomato fruit juice, tomato plants with water, tomato spices, natural soup powder, sodium, oregano, and cumin. Bring to a boil over high temperature, decrease warmth to reduced, and simmer 1 hour, mixing from time to time.

Mix inside coffee beans simmers one hour longer.

Chinese Pepper Steak

Ingredients

- 1 1/2 pounds beef round steaks cut 1-inch thick
- 3 tablespoons vegetable oil
- 1 clove garlic minced
- 1/2 teaspoon salt
- 2 teaspoons ginger root minced fresh or 1 teaspoon ground ginger
- 1/2 teaspoon black pepper freshly ground
- 2 green bell peppers large, thinly sliced
- 1 onion large, quartered and thinly sliced
- 1 (8-ounce) can water chestnuts sliced, drained
- 1/3 cup soy sauce
- 1 teaspoon sugar
- 2/3 cup beef bouillon
- 1 tablespoon cornstarch
- 1/3 cup water cold

Procedure

Place meat inside the freezer for thirty minutes or until the company. Get rid of from freezer, trim away fat, and slice 1/8 -inch thick. Warmth oil in a big weighty skillet or Chinese wok add garlic, meat, salt, ginger, and pepper. Stir-fry over high heat for 4 to five minutes. Remove from skillet and reserve. Add natural peppers and onion stir-fry for three minutes. Return meats to pan and include water chestnuts. Mix collectively soy sauce, sugars, bouillon, cornstarch, and cool water increase meat and veggies in skillet. Mix over high temperature until sauce thickens, about 4 minutes. Serve instantly over very hot rice sprinkle best with green onions.

Codfish Cakes With Tomato Sauce

Ingredients

- 1 cup cod filets flaked, cooked fresh
- 1 1/2 cups potatoes mashed
- 1 egg beaten
- 1 tablespoon margarine melted
- 1/4 teaspoon salt
- 1/8 teaspoon black pepper freshly ground
- 1 tablespoon onions minced
- 1 teaspoon dry mustard
- 1 tablespoon lemon juice fresh
- 1 tablespoon vegetable oil
- 1 teaspoon margarine
- * Part two.
- 2 tablespoons margarine
- 1 onion medium thinly sliced
- 2 tablespoons flour
- 1 1/2 cups tomato juice
- 1/4 teaspoon salt
- 1/8 teaspoon black pepper freshly ground

Procedure

Mix cod, potatoes, egg, 1 tablespoon melted margarine, salt, pepper, onion, mustard, and lemon juice defeat until clean and fluffy. Shape gently into 4 cakes. Sauté in oil and 1 teaspoon margarine until browned. Prepare the next sauce.

Tomato Sauce:
*Melt 1 tablespoon margarine put onion. Sauté until light yellow remove onion. Melt staying 1 tablespoon margarine merge flour and brown somewhat. Add tomato juice progressively and provide to a boil, stirring constantly. Boil five minutes, stirring. Come back the onion to sauce. Include salt and pepper and offer with very hot codfish cakes.

Note: For more proteins, double the quantity of fish in the recipe.

Country Beef Rib Casserole

Ingredients

- 3 pounds beef short ribs cut in serving-size pieces
- 2 tablespoons vegetable oil
- 1 onion medium chopped
- 1 1/2 cups water
- 1/4 cup brown sugar
- 1 tablespoon flour
- Few drops of hot pepper sauce
- 1 teaspoon dry mustard
- 2 tablespoons cider vinegar
- 1 teaspoon lemon juice fresh
- 1 bay leaf
- Salt and freshly ground pepper to taste
- 1 (10 1/2-ounce) package frozen lima beans cooked and drained

Procedure

Heat oven to 325° F. Trim extra fat from ribs brownish in oil. Location ribs in a heavy 2 1/2 - to 3-quart casserole. Drain off excess fat in skillet, reserving about 2 tablespoons. Sauté onion in meats drippings add drinking water and provide to boil. Pour over ribs cover-up and bake for just two 2 hrs, or until nearly tender. Pour off juice into the saucepan and match sugar, flour, very hot pepper sauce, mustard, vinegar, lemon fruit juice, and bay leaf. Bring to boil, stirring continuously, and prepare until well-blended and somewhat thickened. Time of year with salt and pepper pour over ribs and bake, uncovered, for one hour or until meats are tender. Include lima coffee beans cover and bake thirty minutes.

Day-Ahead Brisket

Ingredients

- 1 beef brisket 4- to 5-pound fresh
- 2 tablespoons vegetable oil
- 1 (1 3/8-ounce) package onion soup mix
- 1 onion medium, sliced and separated into rings
- 2 celery medium, chopped
- 1 cup chili sauce
- 1/2 cup water
- 1 (12-ounce) bottle beer

Procedure

Cook brisket until brown on all sides in oil in a Dutch oven. Drain away grease. Sprinkle dried out soup mix over meat. Arrange onion bands and celery at the top. Mix chili sauce and drinking water pour around meats. Protect and bake in a preheated 350° F oven permitting 45 moments per pound cooking period. Baste meat sometimes with sauce. About 45 minutes before the meat is performed, pour beer over best. Continue to bake, protected until meats are cooked. Cool meat in cooking food sauce in the fridge overnight. Remove grease coating. Slice meats and reheat in the sauce to function.

Egg Scramble With Vegetables

Ingredients

- 1/2 pound bacon cut in 1/2 -inch pieces
- 2 onions chopped (about 2 cups)
- 1 cauliflower small, coarsely chopped (about 3 cups)
- 8 eggs lightly beaten
- Salt and freshly ground pepper to taste
- 1 tablespoon soy sauce
- 1 cup Swiss cheese grated natural
- 2 teaspoons chives chopped fresh or fresh parsley (optional)

Procedure

Dark brown bacon and drain in writing towels. Get rid of all but 1/4 cup bacon excess fat from skillet. Sauté cut onions until gently browned add cauliflower items and stir-fry for 5 to 6 minutes. Mix eggs, salt and pepper to taste, soy sauce, grated cheese, optional chives or parsley, and one-fifty percent of the bacon. Pour over combination in skillet and make, stirring, until eggs are usually set. Remove to a comfortable platter and sprinkle with staying bacon. Serve immediately.

Note: This recipe may be used with zucchini, peas and carrots combined, asparagus, corn and limas, or any mixture pleasing to your flavor.

El Paso Tortilla Dinner

Ingredients

- 18 corn tortillas soft, torn into bite-size pieces
- 3 cups chicken cooked and cubed
- 2 cups sour cream
- 2 (10 1/2-ounce) cans cream of chicken soup
- 1 (10 1/2-ounce) can chicken broth
- 1 (4-ounce) can green chilies diced, drained
- 2/3 cup onions minced
- 2 cups sharp cheddar cheese grated
- 2 tomatoes large, peeled and sliced
- 1/3 cup green onions chopped, including some tops

Procedure

In a 9 x 13-inch greased baking dish, layer 1/3 of the torn tortillas, followed with a layer of 1 cup chicken. Mix together 1/2 cups sour cream, chicken soup, broth, chilies, and onion. Layer 1/3 of this mixture over poultry. Continue layering ingredients. Add a final layer of Cheddar cheese topped with tomato slices. Place a spoonful of the remaining sour cream on each tomato slice sprinkle with green onions. (The dinner may be assembled to this point, covered with plastic, and refrigerated several hours if so, add 20 minutes to cooking time.) Bake, uncovered, in a preheated 350° F oven for 40 to 50 minutes or until hot and bubbly!

Eye Of Round

Ingredients

- 1 eye of round 2- to 4-pound
- 1 onion large, thickly sliced
- 1 package au jus gravy mix
- 1/2 cup vermouth
- 2 tablespoons cornstarch
- 1 1/2 tablespoons water cold
- 1/4 teaspoon basil dried, crushed (optional)
- 1/4 cup sour cream

Procedure

Heat oven to 250° F. Place eye of circular in a 1/2 - to 2-quart baking dish. Cover with onion slices. Prepare au jus in accordance with package instructions; blend 1/2 cups au jus with vermouth and pour over meats. Cover and bake for three to four 4 hours. Right before the meat is performed, remove, slice, and maintain hot. Strain juice into the saucepan. Mix cornstarch with 1/2 tablespoons drinking water and mix into sauce alongside optional basil. Warmth, stirring, until obvious and thick. Merge sour cream and function along with meat.

Frankfurter Divan

Ingredients

- 2 (10 1/2-ounce) packages frozen broccoli or 2 pounds fresh broccoli, cooked
- 1/4 cup margarine
- 3 tablespoons flour
- 2 cups milk
- 1/2 teaspoon salt
- Freshly ground pepper to taste
- 3 tablespoons sherry
- 1 cup Parmesan cheese grated
- 1 pound hot dogs all-beef

Procedure

Place broccoli in the greased 8-in . square baking dish. In a saucepan, melt margarine mix in flour and cook, stirring, for three minutes. Add milk and make, stirring, until sauce thickens and starts to bubble. Include salt, pepper, sherry, and 1/2 cup cheese. Remove from warmth keep comfortable. Split frankfurters lengthwise, after that cut in two crosswise arrange over broccoli. Cover with sauce and best with staying cheese. Bake in a preheated 350° F oven for 25 to thirty minutes or until heated through.

Fried Liver With Mustard Sauce

Ingredients

- 1 pound beef liver sliced 3/8 -inch thick
- 1/3 cup flour
- 1/2 teaspoon salt
- 1/8 teaspoon black pepper freshly ground
- 1/2 teaspoon paprika
- 1 tablespoon margarine
- 1 tablespoon vegetable oil
- 1 clove garlic minced
- * Part two.
- 1 tablespoon margarine
- 1 onion medium chopped
- 1 cup water
- 1 tablespoon cornstarch
- 1 tablespoon Worcestershire sauce
- 1 tablespoon Dijon style mustard
- 1 tablespoon dill pickles chopped

Procedure

Cut the liver into helping pieces and pat dried out with paper towels. Mix flour, salt, pepper, and paprika in a pie plate. Dip liver in the blend to coating both sides well. Warmth margarine and vegetable oil in heavy skillet. Sauté garlic until golden. Add liver and brownish quickly, about 2 mins for each part. Remove to a hot platter and keep hot while preparing the sauce.

Mustard Sauce:
*Melt margarine in exactly the same skillet and stir inside onion sauté until cooked through. Mix together drinking water, cornstarch, Worcestershire sauce, and mustard. Blend mix into the skillet and make, stirring, for just two 2 moments. Add pickle and prepare 1 minute. Include liver to sauce and warmth through. Serve immediately.

Ham And Broccoli Dinner

Ingredients

- 2 (10 1/2-ounce) packages frozen broccoli spears cooked
- 6 eggs hard-cooked, sliced
- 2 cups ham cooked diced
- 1/2 pound American cheese grated
- 1/3 cup tapioca quick-cooking
- 1/3 cup green bell peppers diced
- 1/3 cup onions diced
- 1/3 cup celery diced
- 2 tablespoons parsley chopped fresh
- 1/3 cup mayonnaise real
- 1 cup evaporated milk
- 2 (10 1/2-ounce) cans cream of mushroom soup
- 1 cup bread crumbs dry
- 1/4 cup margarine melted

Procedure

Heat oven to 350° F. Grease a 9 x 13-in . baking dish. Cut broccoli spears into bite-size items and spread in baking dish cover up with sliced eggs. Mix ham, cheese, tapioca, green pepper, onion, celery, parsley, mayonnaise, milk, and soup. Pour over contents of the baking dish. Cover with an assortment of bread crumbs and melted margarine. Cover and bake for a quarter-hour uncover and bake for another 15 minutes.

Note: Make forward and remove from the fridge one hour before baking.

Ham And Egg Casserole

Ingredients

- 12 eggs hard-cooked
- 1/4 cup half and half
- 2 teaspoons mustard prepared
- 1/4 teaspoon salt
- 1/2 cup ground ham
- * Part two.
- 6 tablespoons margarine
- 5 tablespoons flour
- 4 cups evaporated milk
- 1/2 teaspoon salt
- 1/4 teaspoon black pepper freshly ground
- 2 tablespoons lemon juice fresh
- dash hot pepper sauce or to taste
- 1 1/2 cups sharp cheddar cheese grated
- Paprika

Procedure

Heat oven to 350° F. Grease a 9 x 13-in . baking dish. Cut broccoli spears into bite-size items and spread in baking dish cover up with sliced eggs. Mix ham, cheese, tapioca, green pepper, onion, celery, parsley, mayonnaise, milk, and soup. Pour over contents of the baking dish. Cover with an assortment of bread crumbs and melted margarine. Cover and bake for a quarter-hour uncover and bake for another 15 minutes.

Note: Make forward and remove from the fridge one hour before baking.

Ham-Filled Acorn Squash

Ingredients

- 3 squash acorn, halved lengthwise
- 2 cups ground ham coarsely
- 1/2 cup celery minced
- 1 apple pared, cored, and finely chopped
- 1 cup crushed pineapple
- 1 tablespoon Dijon style mustard
- 1/2 cup mayonnaise real
- Salt and freshly ground pepper to taste

Procedure

Heat oven to 375° F. Eliminates seeds and membrane from squash. Location cut side straight down on a greased cookie sheet and bake for 45 minutes. Meanwhile, blend the remaining components in a bowl. Divide and location completing squash halves and go back to the stove. Bake for thirty minutes or until squash will be tender.

Ham-Filled Soufflé Roll

Ingredients

- 1/3 cup margarine
- 3 tablespoons flour
- 3/4 cup milk
- 3/4 cup Parmesan cheese grated
- 1/2 cup sharp cheddar cheese grated
- Hot pepper sauce to taste
- 4 eggs separated
- 1/8 teaspoon salt
- 1/4 teaspoon cream of tartar
- * Part two.
- 1 1/2 cups ham minced
- 1/2 cup Swiss cheese grated natural
- 1/4 cup mayonnaise real
- 2 teaspoons mustard prepared
- 1/4 cup onions minced
- 1/4 cup green bell peppers minced
- 1/4 cup sharp cheddar cheese grated

Procedure

Oil the 15 x 10 x 1-in . jelly roll pan making use of sound veggie shortening. Line with foil and oil once again dirt evenly with flour. Dissolve margarine in a saucepan and include flour stir for three minutes. Include dairy continue steadily to make, mixing until thick. Add 1/2 cup Parmesan cheese and 1/2 cup Cheddar cheese mix until melted. Eliminate from heat. Include very hot pepper spices. Beat yolks until solid and lemon-colored beat into the cheese mix. Defeat white wines with sodium and cream of tartar until rigid highs type when the beater is elevated (usually do not defeat until dried out). Flip 1/3 of the whites into cheese mixture to lighten. Fold in remaining white wines until simply mixed. Pass on combination into ready jello roll skillet. Bake in a preheated 350° Farrenheit cooker for quarter-hour or until the surface will be fantastic and company when pushed with a hand. With a spatula, release sides of baked soufflé change on a page of greased foil scattered with staying 1/4 cup Parmesan cheese. Peel from the lime foil from cooked soufflé. Prepare the next filling.

Filling up:
*Mix ham, Swiss cheese, mayonnaise, mustard, onion, and green pepper. Spread surface area of soufflé equally with ham-cheese filling up. Roll-up just like a jelly roll with the help of foil. Location soufflé move seam part straight down on a greased biscuit page. Spread with grated Cheddar cheese. Preheat oven broiler and broil 5 ins from warmth until cheese is dissolved about 4 mins. Serve instantly.

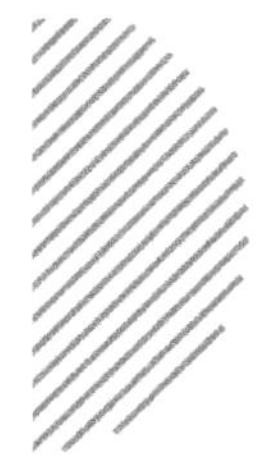